WH Ate The ?

by Matty Long

OXFORD

For Sherman, who also enjoys the odd bug.

OXFORD
UNIVERSITY PRESS

Great Clarendon Street, Oxford OX2 6DP
Oxford University Press is a department of the University of Oxford.
It furthers the University's objective of excellence in research, scholarship,
and education by publishing worldwide. Oxford is a registered trade mark of
Oxford University Press in the UK and in certain other countries

British Library Cataloguing in Publication Data

Data available
ISBN: 978-0-19-277263-3

1 3 5 7 9 10 8 6 4 2

Printed in China

Paper used in the production of this book is a natural,
recyclable product made from wood grown in sustainable forests.
The manufacturing process conforms to the environmental
regulations of the country of origin.

Zzzz.

Greetings. It's me, Snail. I suppose you are wondering why it's dark in here.

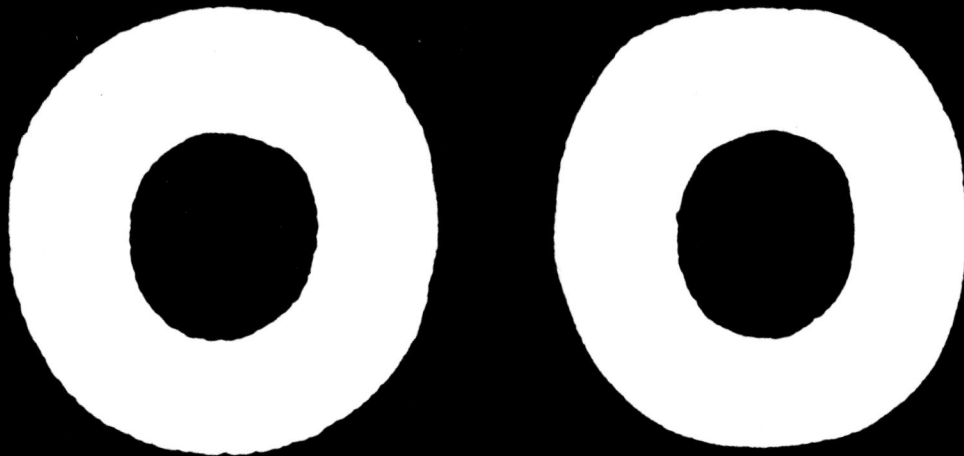

Whee! Boop boop!

And you're probably also wondering who is making that noise.

Allow me to explain . . .

But not everything was rosy in the garden . . .

RUUUN!
Or fly or jump!
Or skitter!

Woooo!
Wheeee!

Being a curious sort,
I decided to investigate.

But nothing would keep me from catching the culprit . . .

But Bird was not to blame.

All the talk of eating had made me hungry. I chewed over what I had learned at the vegetable patch.

Grasshopper tried to talk some sense into me. But I already had another suspect lurking in the long grass . . .

SNAKE! You ate all the bugs. Prepare for JUSTICE!

Bugs? They're more of a snack. I'm looking for something bigger.

Snake wasn't to blame, and I was about to swallow some hard facts.

Spider wasn't to blame. And the biggest shock was yet to come.

I retreated to my favourite thinking rock. It's a hard life for bugs, but without us the world wouldn't be the same.

Finding the bug muncher didn't really matter to me any more.

But then I heard a familiar sound.

Worm always did love hide and seek.
I slid off to investigate . . .

So that's how we ended up here.
There will be no wriggling out of
this one, eh Worm?

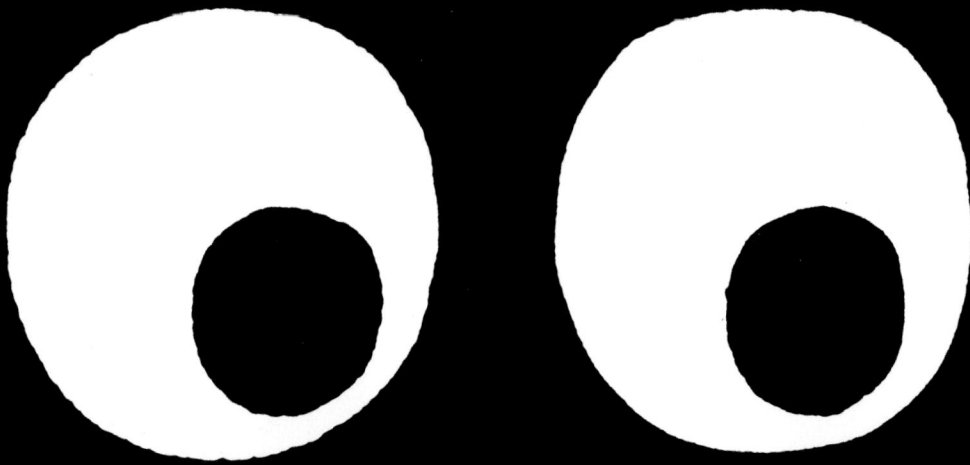

Wheee!

I never did get justice, but I learned that maybe
it was never needed in the first place.
After all, as a wise bug once said . . .

BUGSPLAINING

The term 'bugs' is generally used to describe all kinds of creepy-crawlies. Many of them are insects, but others belong to different animal families. For example, a woodlouse is a crustacean (like a crab!) and a snail is a mollusc (like an octopus!).

Huh?

I am so confused.

GIRL POWER!

Glow-worms are actually classed as beetles, and only the females emit the bright light that gives them their name!

Turn it down!

FAST FOOD

Dragonflies are expert hunters and snatch their meals right out of the sky. They are especially fond of mosquitoes and might eat up to 100 a day!

Well, this sucks.

SPOT OF LUNCH?

The colourful markings on ladybirds make predators think twice about having them as a snack. And if the ladybird is threatened, it secretes a yellow liquid to really put predators off their dinner.

Gross.

MOVING HOUSE

A snail's shell grows with the snail, so they always have a safe place to hide from predators or to stay moist in hot dry weather.

Didn't save me from the frog though!

CURL POWER?

A woodlouse will curl into a ball if threatened, protected by its armour-like shell.

Is it safe to come out yet?

FIGHTS, NOT BITES

Male stag beetles have massive jaws, but they only use them to battle other males. Despite their huge size they don't eat solid food, and instead suck moisture from rotting fruits and tree sap to keep their energy up.

I challenge you to a duel!

Sure!

BEST PALS

Aphids and ants have a special relationship. Aphids suck the juices from plants and create a sticky sweet sap called honeydew which ants can't get enough of. In return, they try to protect aphids from predators.

Don't even think about it!

WORMAZING!

Worms do incredible work around the garden, chomping their way through soil and pooping out nutrients that plants need to grow. Thanks, worms!

Remember, 'phids, it's cool to recycle.

HOPSTARS

Common green grasshoppers can sing for 20 seconds or more!

LA LA LAAAA!

It's a 'no' from me.

Bug Hunt!

You've skittered through the story, but did you spot these brilliant bugs along the way?

COMMON BLUE BUTTERFLY

MARMALADE HOVERFLY

LACEWING

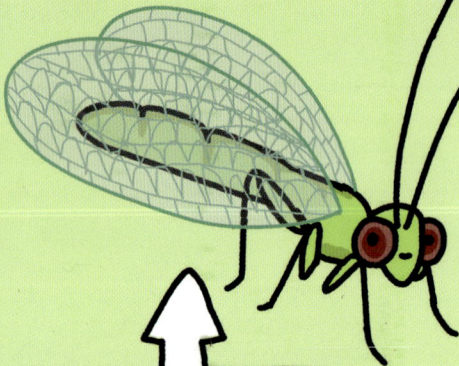

RED-HEADED CARDINAL BEETLE

POND SNAIL

LADYBIRD LARVA

DADDY-LONG-LEGS

YELLOW LADYBIRD

CATERPILLAR IN A PUPA

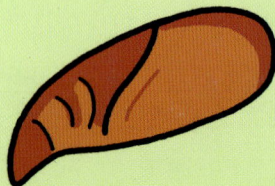

A VERY LONG CENTIPEDE